PIXAR
CAN YOU
SPOT
IT?

AUTUMN
PUBLISHING

WELCOME!

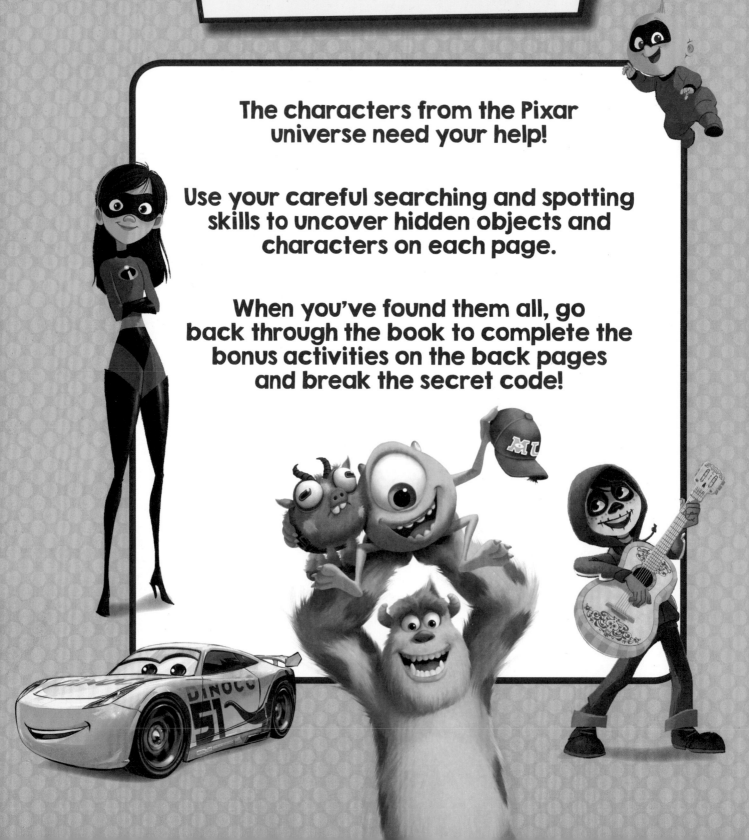

The characters from the Pixar universe need your help!

Use your careful searching and spotting skills to uncover hidden objects and characters on each page.

When you've found them all, go back through the book to complete the bonus activities on the back pages and break the secret code!

Tea Cup Caper

Andy's sister Molly
has invited the toys
to a tea party! Find
**10 Blue Cup and
Saucers** in amongst
the Pixar balls.

WOODY

WHO IS HE?
Cowboy toy

LIKES: His friends, reuniting lost toys with their owners, looking after his kid

DISLIKES: Danger, not being picked to play, feeling useless

QUOTE: "So long, partner."

BUZZ LIGHTYEAR

WHO IS HE?
Space Ranger toy

LIKES: Using his turbo boosters, adventures, his friends

DISLIKES: Crash landings, bullies

QUOTE: "To infinity, and beyond!"

HAMM

WHO IS HE?
Piggy bank

LIKES: Being in charge of the remote control, playing games, looking after loose change

DISLIKES: Losing his cork

QUOTE: "You heard of Kung Fu? Well, get ready for pork chop!"

BUCKET O' SOLDIERS

WHO ARE THEY?
Army men figurines

LIKE: Working together, discipline

DISLIKE: Their cover being blown

QUOTE: "Frag him!"

Disney · PIXAR

REX

WHO IS HE?
Dinosaur toy

LIKES: Video games, working on his roar

DISLIKES: Knocking things over with his tail, arguments, confrontation, Sid Phillips

QUOTE: "The panic is attacking me!"

Lenny

WHO IS HE?
Binoculars toy

LIKES: Warning and reporting while on watch

DISLIKES: Scary new birthday presents, being slow

QUOTE: "Hit the dirt!"

SLINKY

WHO IS HE?
Slinky dog toy

LIKES: Being useful in rescue missions, board games

DISLIKES: Breaking his slink

QUOTE: "Golly bob howdy!"

The Claw

Buzz is playing the Space Crane game! Help him grab **10 Stripy Green and Red Sweets** hidden in amongst the Aliens!

Can you find the Pixar ball?

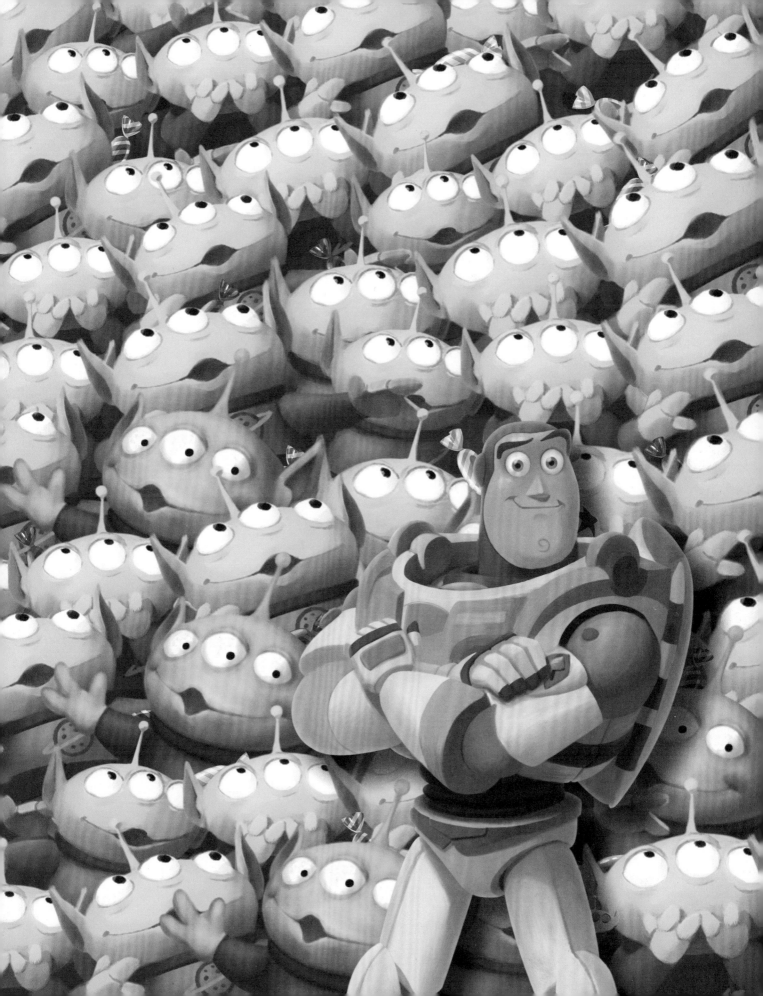

BARLEY LIGHTFOOT

WHO IS HE?
Ian's older brother and magic expert

LIKES: Quests of Yore, Guinevere, adventures, history

DISLIKES: The Growth Spell, Pixie Dusters

QUOTE: "Come dear brother, our destiny awaits!"

IAN LIGHTFOOT

WHO IS HE?
Barley's younger brother and wizard

LIKES: Practising magic, his pet dragon Blazey

DISLIKES: Feral unicorns, his lack of confidence, spells going wrong, Pixie Dusters

QUOTE: "It's not a quest. It's just a really strange errand."

MANTICORE

WHO IS SHE?
Previously fearless warrior, now family restaurant owner

LIKES: Her precious tavern, telling stories from the glory days, her Curse Crusher

DISLIKES: Curses, irritating mascots

QUOTE: "You have to take risks in life to have an adventure."

BLAZEY

WHO IS SHE?
Pet dragon to the Lightfoot family

LIKES: Wrestling with Ian, her lair

DISLIKES: Being squirted with water

DISNEP · PIXAR

ONWARD

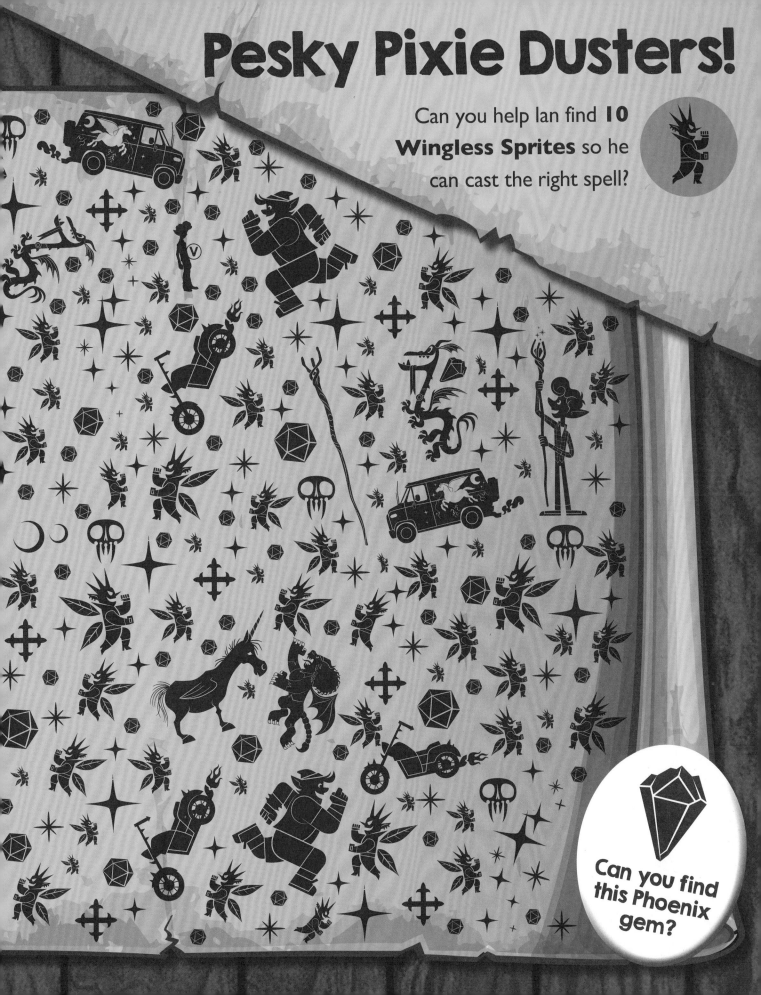

Pesky Pixie Dusters!

Can you help Ian find **10 Wingless Sprites** so he can cast the right spell?

Can you find this Phoenix gem?

The Wheel Deal

Doc has lost some of his **Spare Wheels.** Help him find **10 of them.**

Spot one special tyre like this one!

DANTE

WHO IS HE?
Miguel's loyal companion

LIKES: Bones, food, Miguel

DISLIKES: Ernesto de la Cruz

QUOTE: "Woof!"

HÉCTOR RIVERA

WHO IS HE?
Musician

LIKES: Music, song-writing, his
family, disguises

DISLIKES: Betraying best friends,
being forgotten

QUOTE: "Remember me!"

MIGUEL RIVERA

WHO IS HE?
Future musician!

LIKES: Music, family

DISLIKES: Shoe-making

QUOTE: "Nothing's more important
than family."

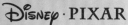
ARLO

WHO IS HE?
Apatosaurus, part-time chicken feeder

LIKES: Berries, fireflies

DISLIKES: Chickens, storms, heights, leeches, lizards, pterodactyls

QUOTE: "I'm done being scared!"

SPOT

WHO IS HE?
Caveboy

LIKES: Corn, berries, hunting, wrestling, scratching

DISLIKES: Pterodactyls, lizards

QUOTE: "Howlllll!"

Musical Mess

Help Miguel find **10 Pink Flowers** in this jumbled pattern!

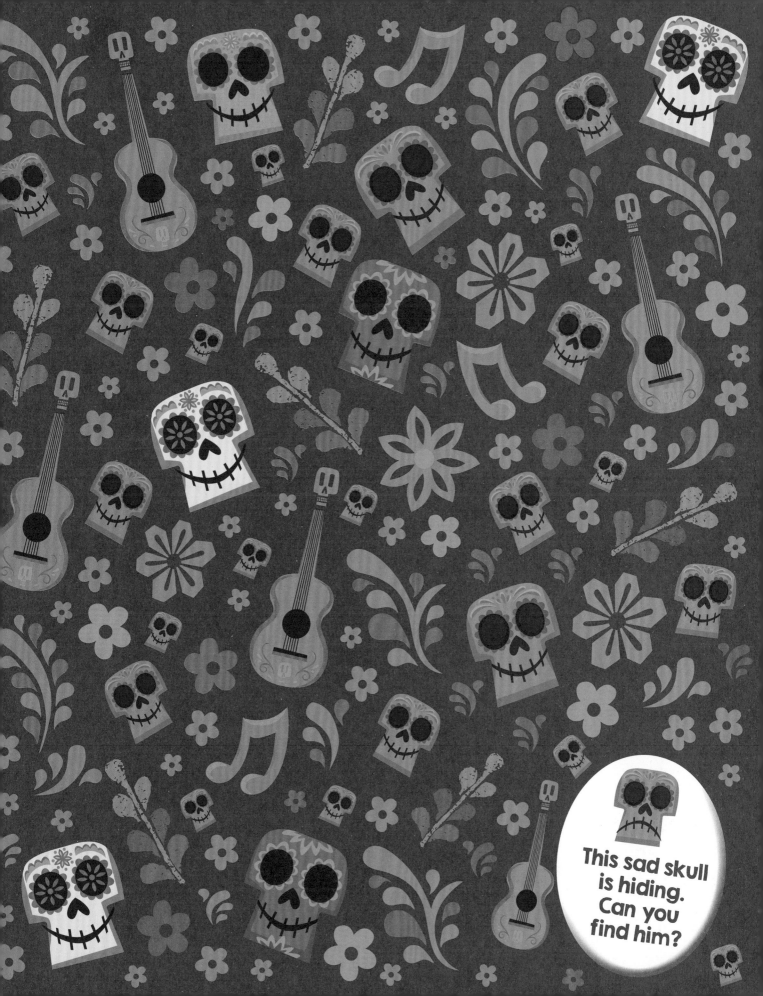

This sad skull
is hiding.
Can you
find him?

Can you find the critter with no nose?

Critter Count

Arlo doesn't like having all eyes on him! Help him find **10 Critters with No Whiskers.**

![Disney · Pixar Toy Story 2 — Jessie hugging Bullseye the horse, with character info cards pinned beside them.]

Disney · PIXAR

TOY STORY 2

BULLSEYE

WHO IS HE?
Faithful horse companion

LIKES: Being loyal to Woody
and Jessie

DISLIKES: Fights, being in storage

QUOTE: "Neighhhh!"

JESSIE

WHO IS SHE?
Cowgirl toy

LIKES: Buzz Lightyear, being in
Andy's room, yodelling

DISLIKES: The dark, confined
spaces (especially cupboards
and boxes)

QUOTE: "Sweet mother of
Abraham Lincoln!"

THE INCREDIBLES

MR INCREDIBLE / BOB PARR

WHO IS HE?
Super and Dad

LIKES: Fighting crime,
the Good Old Days

DISLIKES: Tyrannical bosses,
dead-end jobs

QUOTE: "I mean, who wants
the pressure of being super
all the time?"

ELASTIGIRL / HELEN PARR

WHO IS SHE?
Super and Mum

LIKES: Family, the glory days of
being a Super, flying planes

DISLIKES: Being lied to, flirtatious
mystery blondes

QUOTE: "I think you need to be
a bit more flexible."

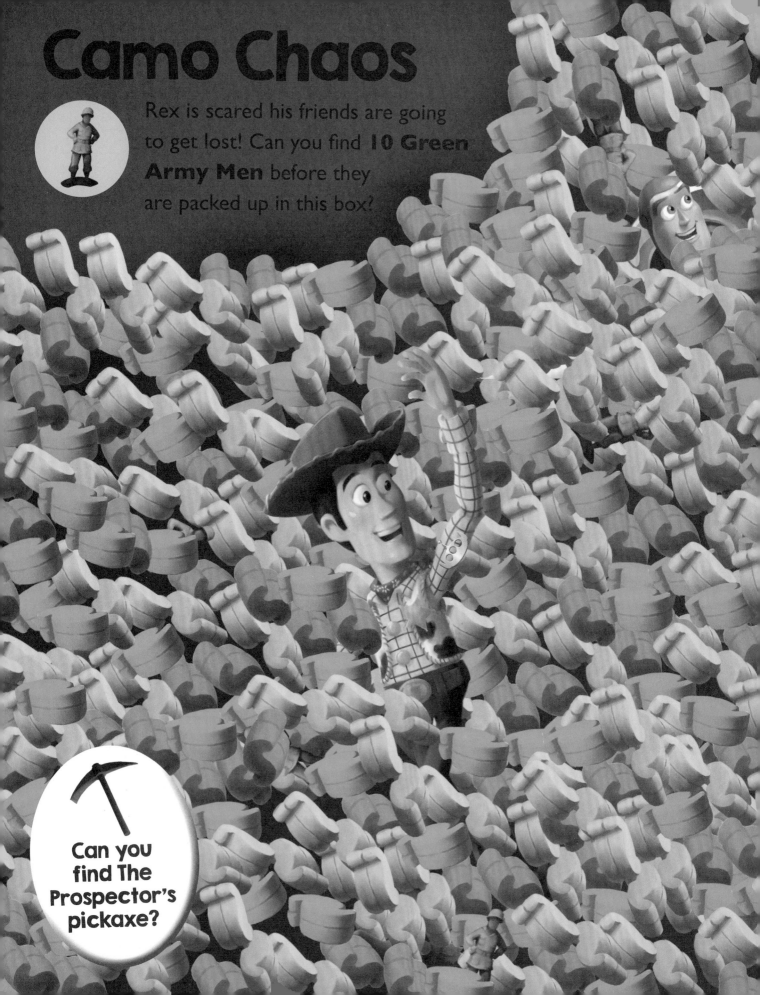

Camo Chaos

Rex is scared his friends are going to get lost! Can you find **10 Green Army Men** before they are packed up in this box?

Can you find The Prospector's pickaxe?

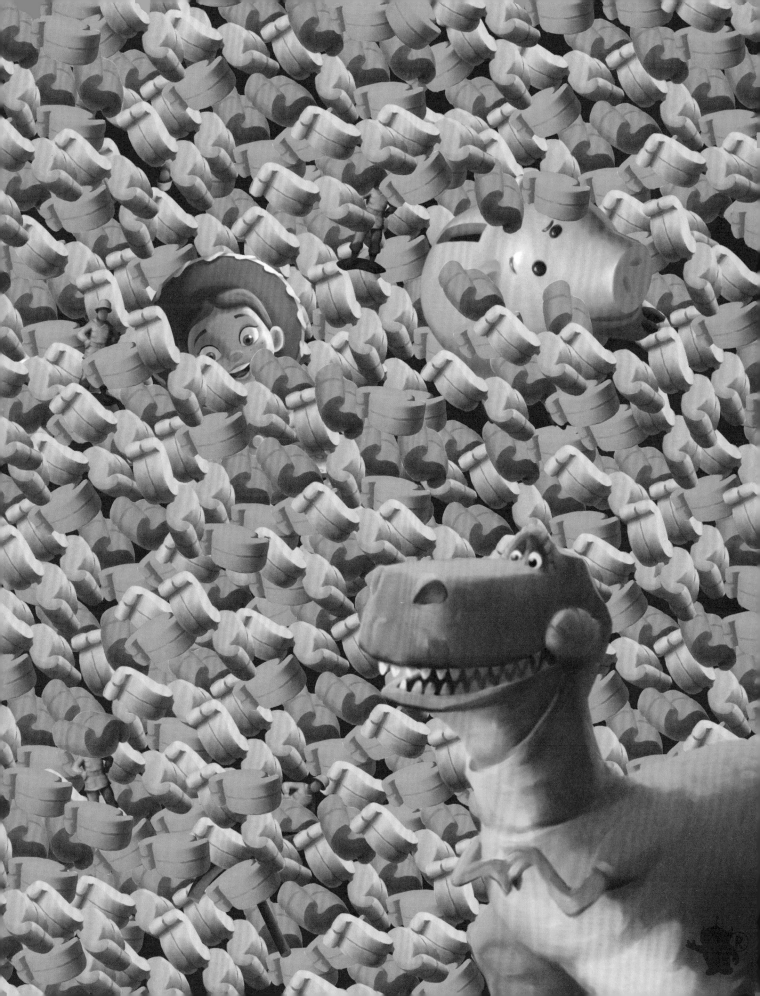

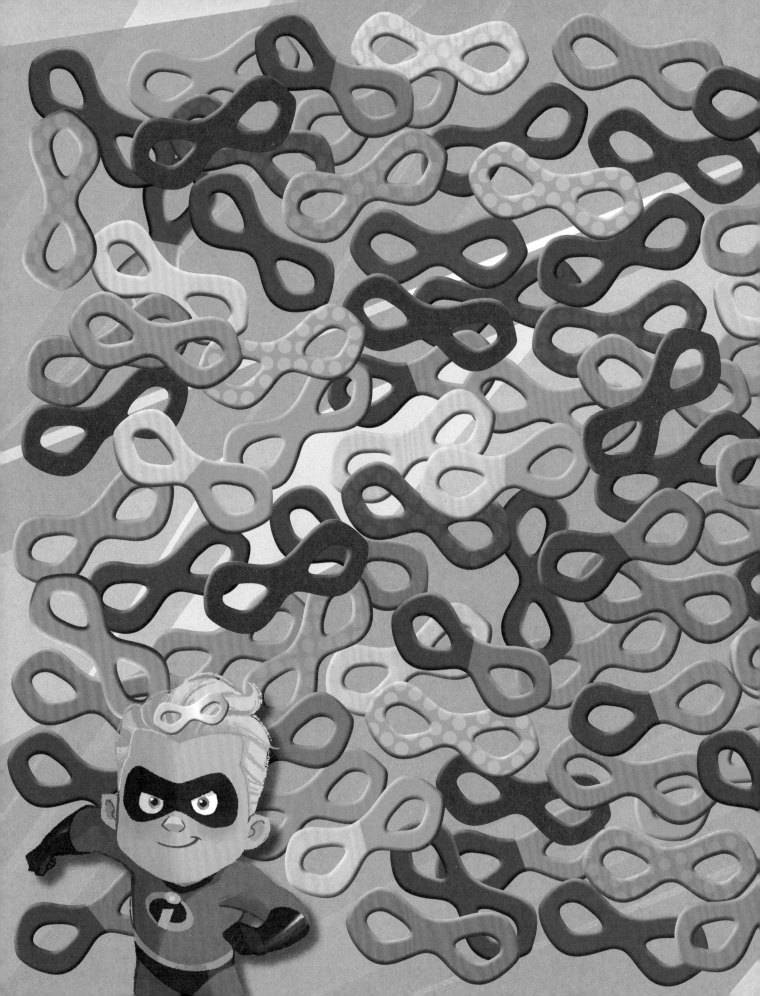

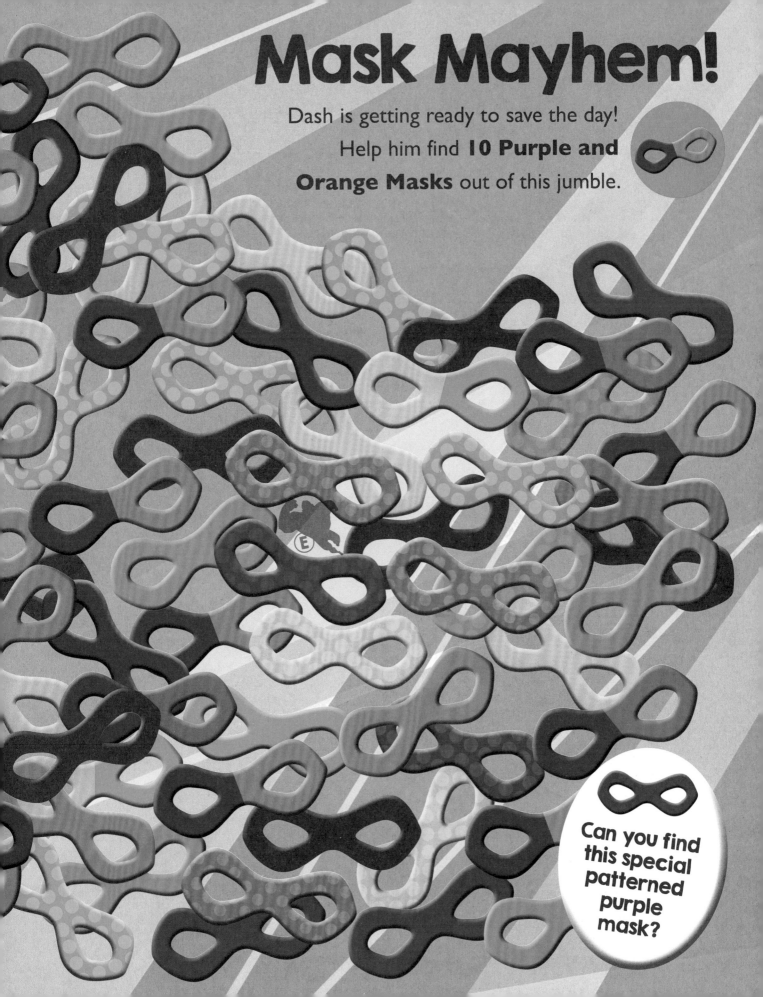

Mask Mayhem!

Dash is getting ready to save the day!
Help him find **10 Purple and Orange Masks** out of this jumble.

Can you find this special patterned purple mask?

NEMO

WHO IS HE?
Clownfish and Marlin's son

LIKES: Exploring, adventures, his lucky fin

DISLIKES: Being lost, scuba divers, tanks, dentist surgeries, Darla

QUOTE: "An anemonemone. Amnemonemomne."

MARLIN

WHO IS HE?
Clownfish and Nemo's dad

LIKES: His safe sea anemone

DISLIKES: Wandering children, boats, seagulls, barracudas

QUOTE: "That's not a duck, it's a... PELICAN!"

Snapshot Spy!

Slinky likes to look back on old times with Andy! Help him find **10 Pizza Planet Logos** in this photo jumble.

Can you find Zurg?

Just Keep Swimming!

Nemo can't find Dory! The **Blue Fish with Two Green Fins on their backs** are the smartest— can you find **10 of them** to help him search for her?

Can you find Dory, too?

DEAN HARDSCRABBLE

WHO IS SHE?
Dean of School of Scaring, Monsters, Inc.

LIKES: Being impressed by the best scarers, no nonsense

DISLIKES: Cheating, rule-breaking

QUOTE: "Keep surprising people."

Disney·PIXAR
MONSTERS UNIVERSITY

ART

WHO IS HE?
New Age Philosophy Major

LIKES: Dream journals, dancing, being a member of Oozma Kappa

DISLIKES: Prison, stinging glow urchins

QUOTE: "I have an extra toe. Not with me, of course."

DORY

WHO IS SHE?
Royal blue tang fish

LIKES: Jellyfish, swimming, speaking whale, shells, family

DISLIKES: Jellyfish... wait, does she?

QUOTE: "Just keep swimming."

HANK

WHO IS HE?
Octopus (ok, fine, a septopus)

LIKES: A quiet, sedentary life, being left alone

DISLIKES: The open ocean, touch tanks, having only seven tentacles, pushing prams

QUOTE: "Holy carp!"

Something Fishy

Dory needs to find **10 Purple Fish.** However, she can't quite remember why...

Nemo is hiding. Can you find him?

WALL·E

Disney · PIXAR

EVE

WHO IS SHE?
Extraterrestrial Vegetation Evaluator

LIKES: Living organisms, flying, WALL-E

DISLIKES: Sudden movements

QUOTE: "Directive."

WALL-E

WHO IS HE?
Waste Allocation Load Lifter - Earth Class

LIKES: Compressing rubbish, collecting knick-knacks, Hello, Dolly!, EVE

DISLIKES: Running out of energy, being electrocuted by AUTO

QUOTE: "EVE!"

CARL FREDRICKSEN

WHO IS HE?
Retired balloon vendor

LIKES: Exploring, adventures

DISLIKES: Being bothered, construction workers

QUOTE: "Let's play a game. It's called See Who Can Be Quiet the Longest."

RUSSELL

WHO IS HE?
Wilderness Explorer

LIKES: Assisting the elderly, chocolate, adventures, nature

DISLIKES: Climbing, losing Kevin

QUOTE: "The wilderness must be explored!"

DUG

WHO IS HE?
Former hunting dog for Charles Muntz, friend of Carl and Russell

LIKES: SQUIRRELS!

DISLIKES: Being called a 'bad dog', the Cone of Shame

QUOTE: "My name is Dug. I have just met you, and I love you!"

Disney · PIXAR

UP

Directive!

Help WALL-E find **10 Forks** on these pages. Watch out for the spoons!

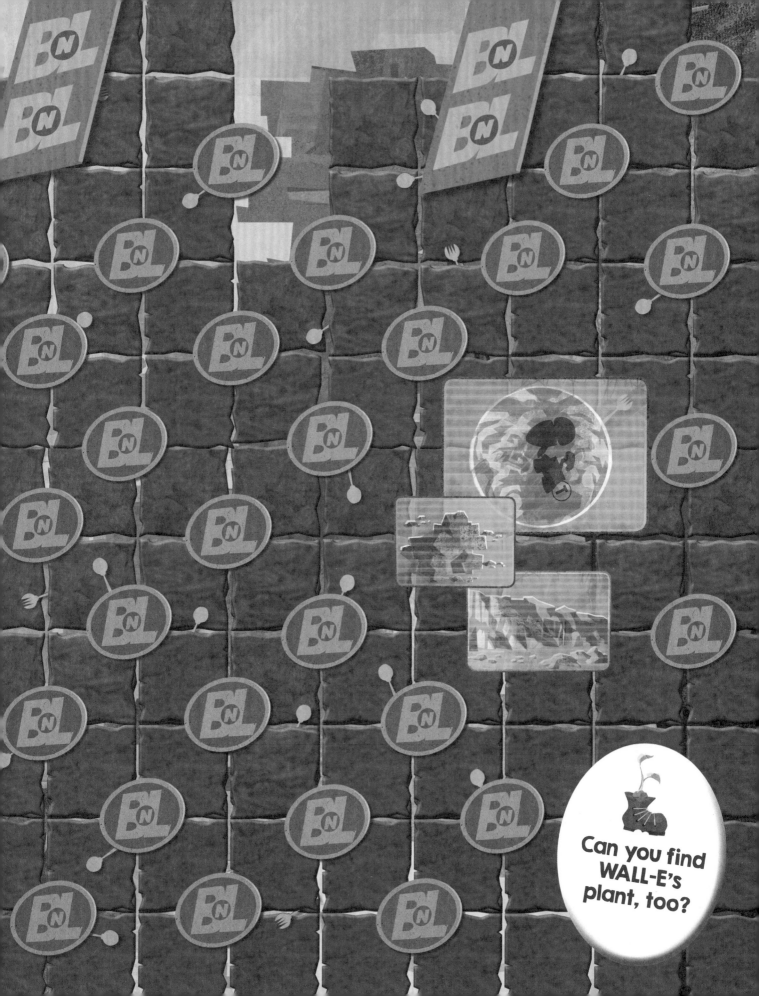

Can you find WALL-E's plant, too?

Can you find Russell's chocolate bar?

INCREDIBLES 2

JACK-JACK

WHO IS HE?
Super-Baby

LIKES: Mozart, cookies

DISLIKES: Being denied cookies, raccoons

QUOTE: "Ga-Ga!"

EDNA MODE

WHO IS SHE?
Fashion Designer

LIKES: Challenges, The Incredible family, babysitting Super children

DISLIKES: Capes, Supermodels

QUOTE: "I never look back, darling, it distracts from the now."

VIOLET PARR

WHO IS SHE?
Student/Super

LIKES: Tony Rydinger

DISLIKES: Attention

QUOTE: "We act normal, Mum! I want to be normal!"

DASHIELL ROBERT 'DASH' PARR

WHO IS HE?
Student/Super

LIKES: Sports, pranks, Sugar Bombs, the Incredibile

DISLIKES: Having to suppress his powers, Maths, detention

QUOTE: "We wanna fight bad guys – it defines who I am!"

Disney · PIXAR

INSIDE OUT

JOY

WHO IS SHE?
Emotion

LIKES: Keeping Riley happy, Goofball Island

DISLIKES: Disorder, Riley being upset

QUOTE: "Think positive!"

FEAR

WHO IS HE?
Emotion

LIKES: Keeping Riley safe

DISLIKES: Boy Band Island

QUOTE: "All right! We did not die today, I call that an unqualified success."

DISGUST

WHO IS SHE?
Emotion

LIKES: Fashion Island

DISLIKES: Broccoli

QUOTE: "When I'm through, Riley will look so good the other kids will look at their own outfits and barf."

SADNESS

WHO IS SHE?
Emotion

LIKES: Reading mind manuals, working together, tragic romance stories

DISLIKES: Not fitting in

QUOTE: "Crying helps me slow down and obsess over the weight of life's problems."

ANGER

WHO IS HE?
Emotion

LIKES: Being angry, reading The Mind Reader, the library of curse words

DISLIKES: Things not being FAIR

QUOTE: "Congratulations, San Francisco, you've ruined pizza!"

Jack-Jack Jumble

It looks like Jack-Jack is showing off his duplicating power to confuse Mr Incredible! Help him find **10 Cookies** before Jack-Jack eats them all.

Can you find the raccoon, too?

Memory Muddle

Joy has got into a muddle!
Help her and the gang find
10 Golden Memories.

Bing Bong is hiding. Can you find him?

CRUZ RAMIREZ

WHO IS SHE?
Trainer and technician at
Rust-eze Racing Centre

LIKES: Racing, being a motivator

DISLIKES: Upsetting others

QUOTE: "Don't fear failure,
fear not having the chance."

MATER

WHO IS HE?
Tow truck, owner of Radiator
Springs salvage centre

LIKES: Tractor-tipping, driving
backwards, playing chess

DISLIKES: Leaking oil, getting wet

QUOTE: "Git-R-Done!"

LUIGI

WHO IS HE?
Owner of Luigi's Casa Della Tyres

LIKES: Ferrari racing, new roads, all
things Italian, white-wall tyres

DISLIKES: Blown tyres, bad tyres,
worn tyres

QUOTE: "Luigi follow only the Ferraris."

GUIDO

WHO IS HE?
Forklift truck

LIKES: Ferrari racing,
pit-stopping for Lightning
McQueen, changing tyres

DISLIKES: When his drill
does not work

QUOTE: "Pit stop!"

Disney · PIXAR

TOY STORY 4

DUCKY

WHO IS HE?
Carnival prize

LIKES: Being in 'Top Prize' spot

DISLIKES: Not being in the 'Top Prize' spot, three-headed sheep, spaceman helmets

QUOTE: "Ooh! So that's what gravity feel like."

BUNNY

WHO IS HE?
Carnival prize

LIKES: Being in 'Top Prize' spot

DISLIKES: Not being in the 'Top Prize' spot, three-headed sheep

QUOTE: "If you think you can just show up and take our Top Prize spot, you're wrong!"

BO PEEP

WHO IS SHE?
Porcelain shepherdess figurine

LIKES: Her friends, herding her sheep, figuring out master plans

DISLIKES: Losing her sheep, antique shops, ventriloquist dummies

QUOTE: "I lead – you follow!"

FORKY

WHO IS HE?
Formerly rubbish, now a full-time toy

LIKES: Bonnie, asking lots of questions

DISLIKES: Walking long distances

QUOTE: "I was meant for soup, salad, maybe chilli. And then the trash! I'm litter!"

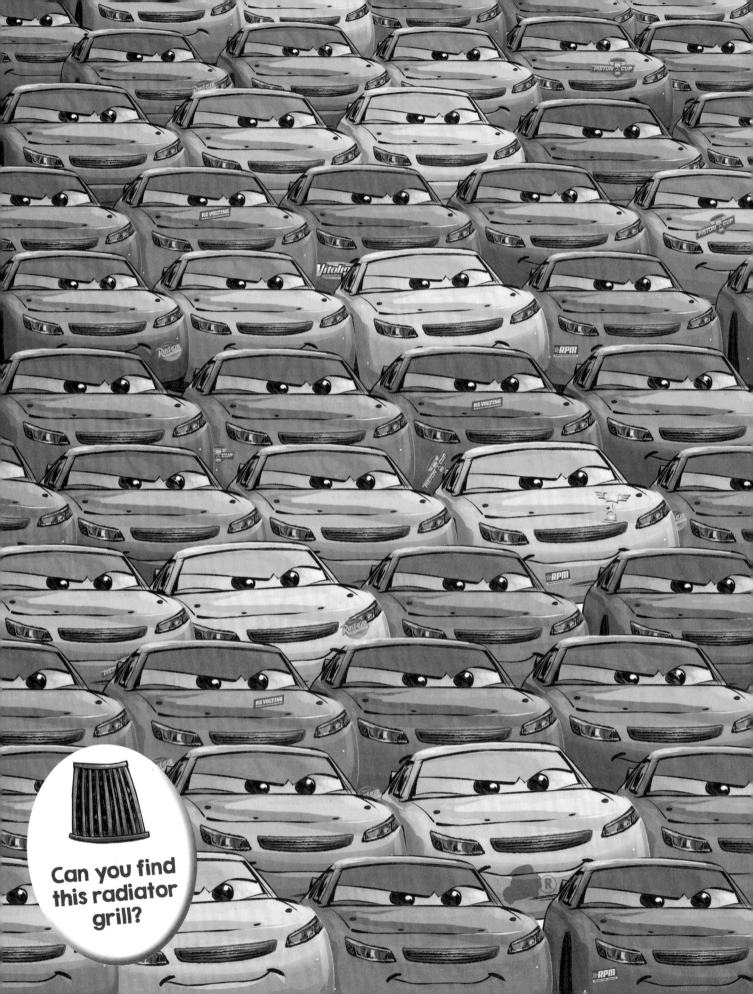

Can you find
this radiator
grill?

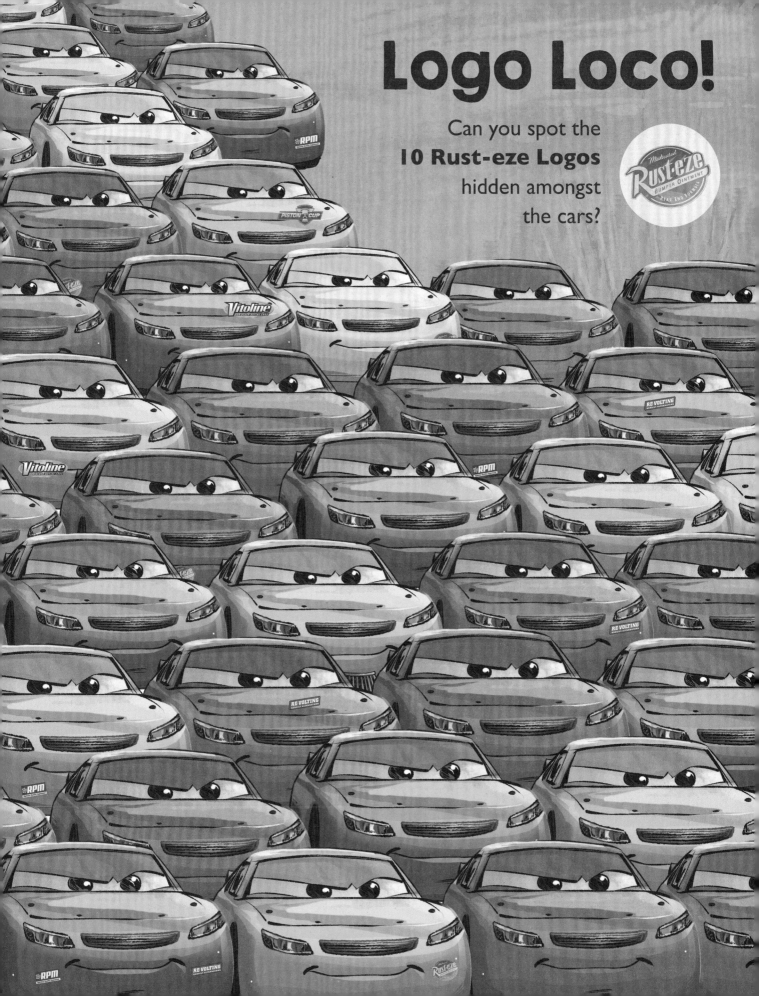

Fun Fair Finds

Woody needs the right rockets! Help him find **10 Blue Rockets with Red Stripes** on this colourful carnival stall!

Officer Giggle McDimples is hiding. Can you find her?

Bonnie has lost her butterfly hair clip. Can you see it?

Bonnie's Beads

Forky needs to help Bonnie find **10 Special Beads** in this arts and crafts pile. Can you help?

CODEBREAKER CHALLENGE!

Well done! Now go back through the book and find all the hidden silhouettes. Once you have found them, write the corresponding letter on the page on the right to reveal the hidden message!

THE GOLDEN ICONS CHALLENGE!

Fancy taking on the Golden Icons challenge? Go back through the book and try to find all of the items below...

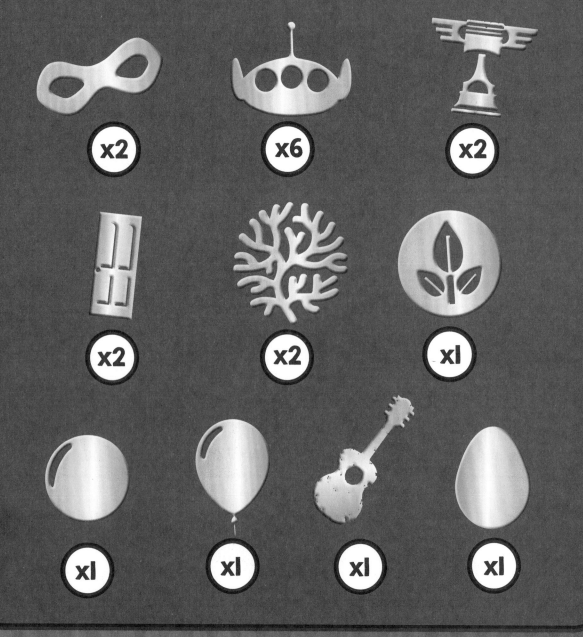